HANDBOOK
for PERFECT BEINGS

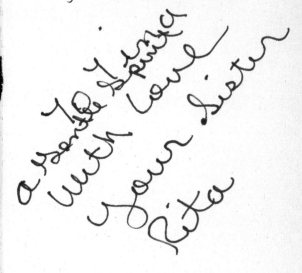

a gentle Tanya
with love
your sister
Rita

Also by B. J. Wall

Guidebook for Perfect Beings

HANDBOOK
for PERFECT BEINGS

B.J. WALL

HAMPTON ROADS
PUBLISHING COMPANY, INC.

Cover design by Rosie Smith/Bartered Graphics
Cover photograph by Steve Wall © 2001

Hampton Roads Publishing Company, Inc.
1125 Stoney Ridge Road
Charlottesville, VA 22902

434-296-2772
fax:434-296-5096
e-mail: hrpc@hrpub.com
www.hrpub.com

If you are unable to order this book from your local
bookseller, you may order directly from the publisher.
Call 1-800-766-8009, toll-free.
Library of Congress Catalog Card Number:
2001091193

ISBN 1-57174-242-5
10 9 8 7 6 5 4 3 2 1

Printed on acid-free paper in Canada

This book is dedicated to Steve—

my best friend, my lover,

my confidant, my husband

Table of Contents

**You are the real
architect and builder
of your life.**

The Handbook for Perfect Beings

The last time I died, on a hot summer day in 1943, it was quite a shock. I was only five years old and it took a while to realize I was dead. My name was Mary Anne and I had been traveling with my family to a reunion in the town of Harrisburg, Pennsylvania. The last thing I remembered was the sound of tires screeching and metal colliding. I was immediately surrounded with complete darkness. An unexpected jerk like a bolt of lightning brought all the senses to attention as my body slammed into a very hard object and landed somewhere in a dream world with a thump. Sharp pain, unlike anything I had experienced before, pierced my whole being.

I began gasping for air. A fear of drowning in this thick darkness and excruciating pain took over. The muscles in my chest felt like a huge elephant was sitting there making breathing impossible. I didn't want to stay in this place. Gratefully, air gradually filled my lungs in huge gulps and calmness slowly replaced the panic.

I realized I couldn't move my arms or legs and my head felt like I had collided with a brick wall. I also couldn't open my eyes for some reason, and so I lay quietly in the darkness, waiting. As my thoughts returned to the accident, I began to worry about the condition of my parents and my older brother. I remembered that my mother and my Sunday school teacher had told me if I was ever afraid I could pray to God and pray I did. Over and over I asked God to help us like a beacon in the darkness. Suddenly, I felt a warmth surround and enclose my entire body. I wasn't hurting anymore. It was as if someone had wrapped me in a warm blanket ever so gently that covered me from head to toe. I seemed to be in the middle of a brilliant light that felt safe and comforting.

Slowly my eyes adjusted to the light and I began to see flowing forms moving on the other side of it. As everything came into focus, the entire scene of the wreck appeared below me. Apparently I was floating right above everything. This certainly was an odd dream. The evidence below confirmed that the two cars had collided at the stop sign. The impact had almost fused both cars at the front sides. Metal, glass, oil, and other car parts were strewn everywhere. Smoke poured from under the hoods of both cars and the smell of burnt rubber was noticeable.

Upon further examination, there seemed to be several people lying on the ground around the wreck. Two of them were immediately recognizable as my parents. My father lay on the ground next to the driver's seat. Pieces of glass glittered in his forehead in a random pattern. A large gash above his left eye produced a swelling of the eye and he was bleeding heavily. The steering wheel had made an imprint on his dark brown suit at his chest. Even though he seemed to be having difficulty breathing, he was alert and asking others to check on his family.

My big brother, Jason, had been traveling in the backseat of the car with me and he was still there. His body was crumpled and his legs twisted like a pretzel. He was unconscious but breathing. I finally saw my mother, who was also on the ground. She wasn't moving and didn't even answer me. I became alarmed when I looked closer and discovered scarlet blood coming from her crushed forehead. Another kind of liquid was seeping out of the same area, sliding down her cheek and hitting the pavement with little splats. She wasn't moving at all.

My attempts to talk to her and the other family members were futile. They either couldn't hear me or just wouldn't respond. At first I was terrified of being by myself. But in the middle of all the confusion, my attention was diverted when an older man from the crowd carefully picked up a little girl. She had obviously been in the wreck and was lying on the ground face down. As he tenderly turned her over, I examined her closely. She had straight brown hair almost down to her waist. Both arms and legs hung limp and useless from her body. She wore a yellow dress with white frilly socks. What used to be blue eyes and a snubbed nose was no longer there. Instead, in their place the skin was peeled back to reveal bones and muscles. The eyes were smashed in toward the brain. To my horror I slowly realized that this was me! But it couldn't be, because I couldn't be in both places at once and certainly wasn't hurting anywhere. I didn't quite understand what dead meant, but maybe that's what happened to me. If this is what it felt like, I didn't like it at all. I realized that I was totally by myself since the others couldn't see or hear me. It slowly dawned on me that I could never go home again or play with my friends. I could never sit in my father's lap or feel my mother's hugs. I began to cry as if my heart had broken. What was happening to my world?

As fate would have it, my mother died in that accident as well. To my amazement and joy she sat up out of her body and stood over it. My crying stopped. It was like she was taking off her dress or slip. She did not accept dying either, but soon became distracted to aid my father and Jason. We followed them to the hospital and stayed with them most of the time. Even though they couldn't see or hear us, we discovered that we could meet them in their dreams and talk and hug just like we used to. Father had a crushed rib cage and a concussion, and my brother, Jason, had broken bones in both legs and his nose. He also had an injury to his neck and had bruised his brain, which caused him to remain in a coma for several days. They both remained in the hospital for several weeks recuperating.

Mother and I took time to watch the people at the mortuary carefully clean and dress our bodies for the funeral. They did what they could to our faces, but the damage had been quite extensive. They dressed us up in our Sunday clothes and attempted to fix our hair. My Grandmama picked out a bright blue dress for Mother that she often wore. I was very happy to notice that my favorite teddy bear was placed with me.

We didn't say much to each other during the process, each of us deep in our own thoughts. It's difficult to describe how it felt to watch people cleaning and dressing your body when you are right there watching.

We also attended the funeral, which was a very interesting process coming from our side. Since I had never been to a funeral, I was constantly asking Mother questions. One of the questions I had asked her about concerned the two boxes placed at the front of the church. She said, "The boxes are called caskets and our bodies are placed in there. That's where we will stay."

This response brought fear to me as I thought about how it must feel to be closed in there. "I don't want to stay in a box forever. I'm scared," I whined. She comforted me by saying that we didn't have to actually get in the box, they only kept our bodies in there. She explained it was a safe place, very much like when she tucked me in at night. That answer seemed to make sense and calmed me.

We sang along with the beautiful songs they played and listened to the minister and friends say nice things about us. We tried to comfort the relatives and friends, but they didn't seem to hear us. The most interesting part of the whole funeral was when they took our caskets to the back of the church to bury them in the graveyard. It was there I discovered many other spirits like us, just sitting on their graves as if they were anticipating something or someone. I finally got the nerve to approach an older man who was patiently waiting next to his wife.

"Excuse me, I was wondering what you are doing?" I timidly asked the man.

I really didn't expect to hear them answer since no one else had heard me. But the old man looked me straight in the eye and to my amazement replied, "She's looking for our daughter. We wait here for our daughter to come visit us. She doesn't come often, but we continue to wait anyway."

"Why don't you go find her?" I questioned.

"My wife is afraid to go anywhere else because she thinks she'll miss her," he replied. "I wanted to leave this place some time ago, but she insists that we be here for our daughter. I'm not going to leave her here alone after all this time, so we both wait."

"I still don't understand why you are stuck here. We've been traveling different places; why can't you?"

"Look around you," he said impatiently. "Do you see all these people just hanging around?"

I saw some people who were wearing strange clothes and soldiers with long guns. Men, women, and children were standing, sitting, or lying on their graves all over the place. The old man explained that most of the spirits were waiting on God to come get them or were stuck waiting on relatives to release them. Still others didn't even know they were dead. They thought they were just dreaming and would wake up someday. It was really fascinating to see all these people waiting to be released or rescued. They were just sitting on their tombstones listening to our funeral, but not noticing each other. The old man, it seemed, knew he could go on, but just wouldn't go without his wife. She kept staring at the gate of the cemetery waiting on their daughter. She felt the daughter still needed her. Her husband was so sad. I was really glad to leave that place.

As Mother and I hung around our old house trying to help with Father and Jason's recuperation, I would often get restless. I had found in the two months since my death that I seemed to be changing. It was like I was growing up very fast. I no longer thought like a five-year-old child, but was beginning to see and remember things as an adult. It was not something I consciously tried to do, but the more willing I was to release old fears and thoughts, the older I got. I also discovered there was another part to this world that I now lived in. We were surrounded by other dead people just like ourselves.

Some of them seemed to be going about their lives just like they did when they were alive. There were mothers still cleaning house, cooking, and caring for their children. There were fathers going to work, mowing the grass, and reading the paper. There were even children who were playing and going to school. Each one seemed to be stuck in their routine and totally unaware that they were now dead.

There were also other spirits who seemed to be wandering, like they were looking for something. All ages and all types of people were constantly traveling in groups or just by themselves. "What were they looking for?" I wondered. I asked Mother about it one day.

She explained, "Some of the spirits are there to help those who were their relatives and friends deal with their death or other problems. Others seem to need to continue with their jobs and everyday routines. Perhaps they don't know they are dead or think the family can't do without them."

That was interesting. Why would these spirits just hang around? Then the thought occurred to me that that was what Mother and I were doing. But why would these people want to continue going to work or school? What about those spirits that seemed to be lost and were wandering? Where do we all go from here? I received my answers from an unexpected source.

It was late one night when Father was having a particularly bad time in his sleep. He constantly relived the accident, blaming himself, so he had some pretty terrible nightmares. Mother and I had been trying to help, but nothing would work. All of a sudden there was this blinding light in the darkness and I saw forms standing around Father. They were gently comforting him and trying to ease his pain.

They were magnificent beings. At first the light was so bright we couldn't look at them directly. The outline of their form resembled our bodies, only much taller. They were completely transparent, yet were filled with this exploding light. I finally gathered the courage to look one of them right in the eyes. My heart seemed to stop. It felt as if they could see right through me and know my thoughts. A voice broke the silence that I could only describe as one having the power of a thunderstorm and the gentleness of a whisper.

Without moving their lips the beings said, "We are your Father's angels."

"That's not possible," I immediately

thought, "because I would have seen you before and I haven't."

They answered, "We have always been here; you just have not seen us."

Now that was not an acceptable answer. There is no way one could miss these brilliant creatures. Yet they explained that I couldn't see them because I wasn't ready to see them. They told me both Mother and I had our own angels. That was difficult to accept, because what did I do to deserve these beings?

"We've always been right beside you," they said, "but your attention has been with your family and friends. You only saw us in your dreams."

Maybe I was looking for the wrong thing. Unlike the Sunday school pictures I had seen, they didn't seem to have wings or halos. They did have these rays of light shooting out of their entire forms. Each one of them reminded me of the bright light of the sun when I would try to look at it directly. After the initial shock, I asked them to answer my questions concerning all the other spirits around us.

They replied, "Some people are just not ready to accept that they have died. Maybe they fear what would happen to them if they did. So they try to feel in control by convincing themselves they will just do everything they normally do and it will be just fine. We try to get their attention, but they won't notice us. Others felt they had to complete something before they could go on. Maybe they needed to tell someone something or try and complete unfinished business.

"Still others seem to be stuck in this world by strong emotions to someone or something. Maybe they were angry with someone or felt they had been cheated or harmed. Often when humans take another's life, the dead souls seem to be attached to their murderers for some time. If they had a strong attachment to a place or a person, they won't leave even after dying. If the human was dependent on alcohol or a drug, they will continue to crave it even in death."

They also talked about the groups of spirits just wandering around in the darkness. They said these beings think they are lost or are expecting some kind of punishment for deeds they performed in life. Often they believe they are in hell when such a place doesn't exist. They are looking for something they couldn't even find while they were alive. Their hope is to find a way out of this place.

One of the angels, named Michael, spoke, "For all of these people who have died, their angels are standing right beside them. It doesn't matter what they are doing or thinking, they have our help. All any one of them has to do is take their attention and thoughts away from the distraction and look at us. That's really all there is to it. They get to choose even in death what they want to do. They can leave anytime. This place they are in is an in-between place for unfinished business. It's not for punishment, but for completion. We have no place of punishment."

Our conversation continued well on into the night. They told me we humans were perfect. I just didn't see how. Since I was being the skeptic, they agreed to show me. That is what enticed me to leave Mother to take care of Father and Jason and go alone with them to a place we call heaven. It seemed like an instant from when I put my small hands in their large ones to when we arrived. In a second we went from a shadowlike darkness that surrounded us to nothing but a ball of glowing light. It was unlike anything I had ever seen. I had to shield my eyes at first because the light took me by surprise. It surrounded everything and was so brilliant it was difficult to look directly at it, just like the sun. The colors of the light would change from pure white to light blues just like the color of the sky on a summer day. This light seemed to be coming from inside of every person and spilled out beyond his or her body. They looked transparent, but everything felt solid to the touch.

The next thing I noticed was all of the activity. It looked like a bee's nest, as people were involved in something everywhere. Some people kept popping in and out like magic. Michael, an angel, told me that traveling in this place was very easy. You just thought about where you wanted to be and you would be there in an instant. He further explained that these people who were popping in and out were probably traveling back to Earth to visit relatives or friends. He also reassured me that I could do the same if I felt my family needing me.

It resembled Earth in that there were buildings, but they seemed to be made of this strange substance that looked solid yet was transparent, just like the people. The rooms were filled with beings like myself and teachers who obviously were angels. The students were excitedly asking questions and talking among themselves. Other rooms were filled with people who were playing music that literally could be heard everywhere, yet there wasn't a microphone or radio to be seen. You heard it with all of your body, not just your ears. It seemed to flow like a river throughout your body, healing everything it touched.

There were fields of flowers of every color and type in perpetual bloom. You could pick one and another took its place. There also were trees, large enough to provide shade and yet small enough for children to climb. Deep blue rivers flowed in, out, and around the buildings and people.

Animals and children romped in the fields together and played in the water, oblivious to others around them. There were people everywhere and each had their own angels with them and the conversations included everyone.

I noticed artists who were painting, sculpting, drawing, and creating. A large clear sphere emerged where, I was told, people were learning about future inventions. It was huge, much larger than anything I had ever seen. The sphere was totally round, like a large crystal ball, and yet there were different rooms throughout that just seemed to hang in the air all by themselves. People and angels were huddled in various sections, totally involved in their studies. In the very middle of all of this activity there were groups of people talking, laughing, and reuniting.

I noticed additional people on the outskirts of this heaven who seemed to be in their own little world. They didn't seem to notice all the activity going on right beyond them. They were fervently building places of worship, busy arguing philosophy, and trying to find places for themselves in this new world. I asked my angel John what was going on.

He explained, "These are people who are busy creating what they think heaven is supposed to be. They aren't ready to let go of their preconceived ideas of what it's supposed to be and aren't ready to accept new ideas. They will tire of this at some time and be willing to join the others. They think their connection to God can only be found in buildings or ceremonies. They don't understand that they are the connection, not the building."

I looked even beyond these people and to my surprise found others that seemed to be asleep. Their angels were patiently waiting right beside them for them to awake.

"What are those people doing?" I questioned.

"They are asleep because they had such a difficult time in their last lifetime, the soul needs to rest. The whole time they are resting, they are receiving what they think are dreams. These dreams are really messages to prepare them for the rest of heaven," replied

Jonah, another one of my angels. That seemed to satisfy my curiosity.

At first, I spent some time with my angels at a very special place that looked like a small room with a huge screen. We were alone, yet I knew that others were around us doing the same thing. I couldn't see them and they couldn't see us. We watched the screen together and saw each of my lives and even the times in between, one at a time. It was most interesting and my angels patiently answered all my questions. Often I would ask them to stop the picture so that I could remember and feel what the other people in my life were feeling. Sometimes it hurt so much it felt like that pain I experienced at my death. And yet, other times it was so exciting and joyful. My angels told me it was like having a reunion with myself. All in all we watched twenty-two lifetimes, including the one I just left. I was speechless.

The angels explained that the purpose of reviewing all the lifetimes was to give me a better understanding of why I chose the things I did and who I really am. Until you see this, you can't see all parts of yourself in order to make better decisions in future lives. I asked them when would I be judged? Mother and others had told me throughout my life when I was bad I would be punished. I knew I had more than a few "bad" experiences and assumed I would have to pay dearly. Michael looked at me very surprised.

"There is no punishment here, only understanding. Why would we punish you for trying to learn about life and yourself? In looking at your different lives and feeling what others felt, as you have just done, you simply have a more complete understanding of who you are," explained Michael. "If God created you perfect, how could anything be wrong? Since God doesn't judge you, why should anybody else?" I was quickly relieved, as that made sense.

We gradually made our way to several of the classrooms going on near a lake. I recognized several of the people who had been in my past lives and decided to join in their conversation. They were talking about Universal Laws and how they related to us.

I didn't ever remember hearing about Universal Laws, yet, strangely I understood what they were saying even as it came out of their mouths. These were the guides for the universe created especially for us and I had to know more. I knew this was the truth as I had never experienced it. I quietly listened as every law came back to the fact that we each were perfect. Having just returned from revisiting all my past lives, I still didn't see how.

Many questions were asked and answered before the group broke up. I was so hungry to hear more that I kept walking until I found another group talking about these same things. I learned in this group there are eight Universal Laws. They are:

1) You are cocreators with God and are creating your own life

2) When you create you do it in circles or cycles

3) The Law of Cause and Effect—only choices

4) There is no good or bad—just opposites

5) Judgment—there isn't any

6) All beings have angels to help them

7) Perfection is the combination of your opposites and the acceptance of both

8) All paths eventually lead to the same place; why not enjoy the trip?

I went through several classes to get as much information as possible. I knew as I heard it that what I was being taught was the truth. I wanted very much to remember it. But how?

I met with numerous people to decide when and where to reconnect with them in this next life. Using all the information I had received, I based my sex, race, culture, parents, lifestyle, and direction on what I wanted to learn this time. I chose my parents because they would remind me of the strengths I wanted to keep and the weaknesses I wanted to understand and change. I knew what I needed to do this next time and I wanted to remember as much as possible. When I decided on the parents and direction of my life, I started visiting the womb. It was quite cozy, but I didn't want to stay there. I would go back and forth from the womb to heaven continually, trying to memorize as much as possible of the Universal Laws. Just before the time of my actual birth, Michael handed me a small, worn book. I was really surprised; a gift? On the cover it was entitled *The Handbook for Perfect Beings*.

"What is this?" I asked.

"It's what you have been requesting," answered John, an angel I was the most familiar with. "It's a book to help you remember how to get back to who you really are. You are going to get caught up in simply living while you are down there. Sometimes it's not enough that we are with you. Sometimes you need more. Every being gets a copy of this book at one time or another. It's your time. Also, you will be able to see us this time, which should help you."

I carefully examined the book and discovered all the Universal Laws were in there, as well as answers to most of the questions I had heard in the groups. I spent the last few hours before birth trying to memorize my book. Finally the time came.

As I felt myself being squeezed out of this very narrow opening, I kept saying to myself, "Remember the book, remember the book, remember the book."

Well, it's taken fifty years for me to remember the book totally. Pieces of it came a little at a time. Sometimes it came through the words of others. Sometimes it was through life experiences. Most of it came through me as I channeled angels in groups or individual sessions. The refining of the material has come as I have spent a great deal of time listening and talking to my own angels. They have been so important to me in this life. It did help that I could see them and talk to them. But I, like everyone else, have had periods in my life when I still felt alone. They've helped guide me and best of all remind me constantly of how perfect we all are. I originally had four angels to help me and now I have twelve. They are the true authors of this handbook so I take little credit. What follows in the remaining pages is the original *Handbook* that I was given. It is in their words, not mine. The Universal Laws will be stated at the beginning of each chapter. Their answers to possible questions will follow. You will notice that they often refer to problems surrounding finances and relationships as examples. These two areas seem to be the most difficult for us humans to change. So they have approached these problems with new ways to see and handle them. They will refer to God as the Creator or simply They to indicate that God is all-inclusive and is neither a he nor a she. Let it change your life as it has mine.

Be Aware!

Once you have started the journey, you can never go back to the place of unknowing where you are now residing. But then you probably wouldn't want to.

When we make
a request from God,
we aren't testing God
but our own limits
and boundaries.

You Are Cocreators with God

Whether or not you recognize or understand it, you have the ability to create your life every day, every moment. You are doing this either consciously or subconsciously, but you are definitely doing it. You are creating through your thoughts, words, and actions just like the Creator created the entire universe. This isn't a gift; it's your birthright that's part of your soul and always connects you to your partner—God.

A Sense of Order

All the way back to the beginning, creating was never a chore. It was never difficult because God felt it was an expression of love to create these things to see and enjoy. The desire to share this creative ability with all parts of Their creation was never in doubt. The question was simply how. So God quietly planted the ability to create in each being's soul. So you inherited it, very much like a spiritual DNA. There needed to be a sense of order to this creating, so the Universal Laws were developed and put into place. They were fairly simple ones, but the difficulty came in when you forgot them. Each time you came back in a different body and settled down to experience living, you forgot a little bit more.

This order always exists, regardless of what you are creating and even if you don't understand it. Often what you notice first are the effects or consequences of what you created. Even when you feel your life is in total chaos, there is an order to it. You just aren't seeing it. The first Universal Law says if you can recognize that you are the creator of the chaos, then you certainly have the power to change it.

Think of it as similar to a tornado. The outside winds are a whirlwind of destruction, yet there is calm at the very center. That is where your true power lies. If you can get to that power in the center, you can be at peace no matter what is going on around you. So there is order. It doesn't matter what you believe. It doesn't matter what your religion is. It doesn't even matter what planet you are on. It's simply there and it works. It always works.

How Do You Create?

You create just as the Creator does, through your thoughts, words, and actions.

You think that those thoughts in your head are simply a flow of endless words. Sometimes you share them with others, but most of the time you don't. Either way it is hard to realize that you're creating with thoughts because they are so random. They just tend to constantly react from one situation to another every day.

If you can start to see that you are controlling your life with every thought that leaves your head—even the random thoughts—you are reclaiming order in your life. For instance, let's say you are driving down the highway. You start to become very aware of other drivers who are rude and slow you down. You really are creating the situation and are literally pulling them toward you by your thoughts. The more you concentrate on the fact that these people aren't very considerate, the more upset you get. The angrier you get, the more you attract these drivers to you. You are creating your own whirlwind. You can stop this kind of situation by simply letting the original driver who irritated you go and not responding.

Building or Tearing Down

You really are the architect and builder of your life. Your thoughts are creating your life moment by moment. They are either building what you want or tearing it down.

Since thoughts create, when you are thinking about something you are literally building it right in front of your eyes a piece at a time. Your thoughts are like the design or blueprint and your words and actions actually build it. What usually stops you from achieving what you want is a narrow idea of what it's supposed to be and how it's supposed to happen. Sometimes after you have a request or an idea, you begin to doubt or change your mind. When you do that, you are, in effect, taking a sledgehammer to your original thought or request. Then you get upset because it didn't happen and begin to blame everything around you, including God.

This whole thing isn't about proving yourself to God or even for God to prove anything to you. It's all about proving just how powerful you are to yourself.

Think about it. The Creator already knows everything there is to know about you. Why would They need to have you prove something They already know? This same Creator sees you as perfect and wants to give you all the resources available throughout the universe. You are the one who stops it. So simply take God out of it and look at what limitations you hold on to that are stopping you from receiving what is yours. You are the one who doesn't answer your own prayers or requests.

You stop it in one of several ways. Most often you stop the request by thinking or saying something that discredits your ability to make it happen. Often you might say, "That's impossible," or "It probably won't happen to me." What you're really saying is that you don't think you are worthy of the request. Even saying, "If it's God's will," puts the control for it to happen entirely in the Creator's hands when you are the original creator.

If God had installed a merit system, many people would be in trouble. They would be forced to spend their entire lives trying to figure out what the system is and how to earn it. If this merit system existed, then all parts of creation would be forced to live by it. Look at nature. Are some plants more worthwhile or enjoyable if they are bigger or better? Does the sun or the wind have to earn God's approval? No. Each has its place in creation and is unique.

Another way you limit yourself is to think that the answer to your request has to come to you in certain directions. Take, for instance, a request for increased finances. Most humans believe that money can only come through their job, relatives, friends, or winning the lottery. So as soon as the request is made, you try to figure out which direction the money might come from. Since these are the only directions you are looking for, you probably will miss it.

Another limitation is that your request has to look a certain way. If you asked for a new car, you might not be looking for a car that's new to you but is not necessarily the most recent model. Most people want to believe they are all entitled to the same things in life. They work very hard to achieve this goal, usually relinquishing their power to others in the process. If what you are looking for is great riches, big houses, or expensive cars, you aren't going to notice all the gifts you've received from Creation along the way. Your original request probably isn't going to look like you thought it would anyway.

To receive what you have asked for, it is first important to see yourself as working with the Creator as a partner. See yourself as powerful enough and worthy enough to receive it. Second, break away from your limited ideas of what it is supposed to look like and how it's supposed to come. All you need to do is make the request, see the end result you want, and thank the universe for it. It isn't necessary to spend time trying to figure out how it might come or what you need to do. If something comes to your mind that you strongly feel you need to do concerning the request, that's fine. If nothing comes, release it and give thanks. That is how simple it is to create.

There is a system of
order to the universe
and everything in it—
including tornadoes,
hurricanes, and floods.

Everything Travels in Circles

*Every thought, word, or action
travels in circles. You already know
this, as you are constantly reminded to
be careful what you ask for because you
might get it. Your thought or word
reaches out, touches others, and returns
to you much stronger than when it left.
If you truly realized the power of this,
you would be more careful about what
you think, say, and do. The idea is not
to punish you, but to help you see and
recognize what you are creating.*

Basic Explanation

All parts of creation travel in some form
of a circle or a cycle. From the smallest atom
inside you to all the planets in the universe,

they all travel in circles or cycles. Therefore it makes sense that the most basic rule says that whatever you are creating goes out and returns to you. It has no choice.

Sometimes humans get confused when "bad" things seem to happen to "good" people. Sometimes it also looks like people who hurt others get rewarded in return. Where you get stuck is your interpretation of what is being sent and what is returning. Your uniqueness gets you in trouble. The way you think the world is supposed to be isn't going to be the same for everyone else. It's uniquely your opinion. Since everything, including growth, has to go in circles, humans have to experience both pain and pleasure before they can fully understand what it is they are trying to figure out. You have to visit both in order to be able to see more of the picture. Since you can't possibly understand everything involved in that situation, your interpretation of what is happening is going to be limited at best. Maybe that person chose to experience that particular lesson in order to have a clearer understanding of something they were dealing with.

Why should this be important to you? Even though you can't actually see the circle, accepting that it will happen is the second step in regaining your power to create what you want. It gives you the ability to actually stop yourself and be in control of where you want to be instead of just reacting.

How to Change Your Finances

One of the most difficult circles for humans to understand is finances. That's where you get stuck so quickly. For example, you have a big bill due and you are very worried about it. Your first thoughts are "Where am I going to get the money to pay this bill?" You are also thinking of the consequences of not paying that bill and fear starts to grow. Maybe it's late charges you're afraid of, or that they might shut your power or phone off. You could worry that it's going to hurt your credit or what would other people think.

When you do that, the thought that you do not have the money to pay this bill goes out. The very second that thought leaves your mind, the circle starts. The more often the thought goes out, the more it comes back to you again and again as the fear grows. Eventually you're focusing on nothing but the fear and you feel trapped. You not only are creating exactly what you don't want, but you are also bringing it right back to you. What you have done is literally create the scenario that you didn't want in the first place. The more often you think about this, the quicker you create it.

Why not create what you really want instead? Remember you are the one doing it and you have choices. By choosing to change the fear to peace, you are taking control of what you want to see in your life. So let's take the same example and turn it around. Let's say you have your bill and your checkbook in front of you. You think the bill and your bank account are real because you can see and touch them. They are merely symbols. The only thing that's real is what you're creating in your head. Why limit the amount of money you have available to only what's in the bank? Your first impulse might be to say, "I don't have

the money; how am I going to do this?"
The way you change the situation is to stop
and say, "I have all that I need to take care
of this and more and I'm grateful." See your
bank account as full and send out that bill
with joy. See the circle of it all as it helps
others to feed their families and pay their
bills.

You can do this in your head even if
your mind wants to say, "Wait a minute.
You're trying to fool yourself; you can't
spend what you don't have." You are the
one in charge of your mind. What you're
hearing are old tapes. So choose to change
it. Look at your checkbook and the bill and
tell yourself this is simply a symbol. Money
is really just a piece of green paper. If you
don't understand that you are the one creating it, then you are giving that piece of
green paper every bit of your power.

Stop and say, "I know that I have everything I need to take care of this and more,
thank you." See yourself gladly writing the
check and sending it off, having plenty left
over. What you've done is create another
circle. By seeing the end you really want,

you're bringing the consequences of that circle back to you. You're just choosing to focus on the peaceful route instead of the fearful one.

Take the last thirty minutes. Think back to what you were thinking. We're not saying that you have to consciously monitor or filter every second. We are saying start to be aware of your power. Take this very thing you've inherited from your Creator and use it to your advantage. Whatever you were thinking about in that thirty minutes is what you were creating. The ability to create is centered on the fact that if you focus on it long enough, it becomes reality. Just as in the example about finances, you have started building whatever it was you were thinking of. If you're worrying about something for minutes or even days, you are literally creating whatever it is that you don't want. You shouldn't be surprised when it happens. According to the Universal Laws it has to.

Even when you do try and change your thoughts, you have limits and expectations. If it doesn't happen by your deadline, doubt creeps in. It isn't very long before the doubts start to interfere with your circle to change it. Then when it doesn't happen by the end of the second week, you rationalize that something went wrong. Or you might say that it probably wouldn't happen to you anyway.

When you have a thought that you are being punished or made a mistake, you literally go and kick down whatever had been created. It's like taking a sledgehammer and destroying it, because your mind is what creates it, absolutely and literally. Often it's not going to happen as quickly as you want because it's dependent on a lot of factors. This is true especially if it's involving other people; it has to connect with them too. They have a right to choose too.

Remember, how you send your bills out certainly affects how the money comes back to you. If you send your money out grudgingly, all the while seeing your checkbook balance disappear, that's exactly what you will get. But if you see your bills as part of a circle that helps others, and your money returning in greater amounts, you are releasing the power of money. The more things that can leave your mind with joy and thanks, the more you're going to get back. The rewards are not just money or things, but a sense of freedom. You begin to realize that you are the creator of this. You're entitled to both needs and pleasures in life; it's your inheritance. Anyone can take an inheritance and squander it. It isn't the amount of money you do or don't have; it's how you perceive it.

So if you want to change things, just simply know that the money you need is there. Even when it looks like everything is going wrong, see the circle. Hold to the fact that everything is perfect and you have no choice but to create perfection. Being able to sit in the middle of a whirlwind or storm and have peace is what this is all about. That is the ultimate knowing. That's what everyone is looking for. It's not just the answers to questions, but how you get to a place where you can see your choices and choose wisely.

We are not suggesting that you quit your job and spend all your time meditating or just thinking about your needs. You will probably need to work for what you want. But we are saying that you can start to be aware of your thoughts and beliefs about your ability to access all the benefits of the universe. Start to be aware of how often you define yourself by your job and your finances. The acceptable belief is that if you have lots of money, you are successful and are being rewarded by God. If you have little or no money, you must be experiencing punishment from God for something you did.

There is no reward and punishment. There are only opportunities to experience lessons in reclaiming your power from the green paper you call money.

There are no such things as accidents or coincidences.

The Law of Cause and Effect

The Law of Cause and Effect deals with the end result of the circles you have created. It states that for everything you do, say, or think there is an effect that is going to return to you. It also says that every time the consequences or effect of something you have created comes back to you, you have an opportunity to do one of three things with it. You can either keep it the same, change it, or release it. One of these three choices is made every time you find the same things happening in your life.

Karma is a part of cause and effect. Humans often use the word without understanding what it means. It basically says that if you have said or done something that affects others in your life, your actions will eventually come back to you. So what you're probably going to notice first is the effect. You then make one of the three choices. Depending on which choice you make, you create yet another effect. For instance, if you harmed someone in the past, one way to understand that harm is probably to experience it. The idea is that you then can be aware of both harm and love, which are balanced. Then you have a chance to release it or change it. If you keep reacting emotionally to the situation as a victim or blaming others, you are keeping it. But if you decide to get out of the emotions and ask what you can learn from it, then you are able to change it or even release it.

If you harmed or killed someone in a past lifetime, the best way you're going to understand what that person felt would be to go through the experience yourself. But the whole idea is not to stay stuck with the experience. Many humans believe it's been refined to a debt system where, if you harm or hurt others, you have this debt you will have to pay back. We're saying don't keep it there. That's only half of it. The other part is that you incorporate that experience into your life to try to understand what it was about so you can change it. So the purpose of the effect of that situation is to help you to understand what it felt like, incorporate it, and change it.

Where most people get stuck is staying emotional about things that seem to be unjust or unfair. You are really each other's teachers. Often you meet someone in life that simply drives you crazy. It can be that you really like them or you really don't, either way. If you feel very strong emotions toward someone or something, it's probably very old and it's there for you to learn from. The idea is not to stay stuck in those emotions by the way you react to this person. To get past being stuck, you simply ask, "What is it that I'm supposed to learn without actually having to repeat that situation again?"

Lessons

If you are constantly worrying about what you're thinking or doing, you're actually creating the effect you don't want. If you are someone who constantly worries about what other people think of you, you are stuck. You're worrying about the effect. If your intentions are pure, then you just let it go. Release what you have said or done and let it be taken as it needs to be and let them react. If it has not been a pure thought or word and you're not comfortable with it, you will know the effect is going to come back to you. Then you simply forgive yourself and find out what you want to change the next time.

That's it.

It really isn't more complicated than that, because you can drive yourself crazy sitting around worrying about every thought or word that comes out of your mouth.

Sometimes you subconsciously agree to be part of a learning experience with others where you aren't the one setting up the karmic affect. You simply are part of the situation as their partner or teacher. For instance, you could be involved in a car accident and hurt someone unintentionally and you would probably feel very guilty about it. But if you could try to understand what is really happening before you attach guilt, you will release yourself from their lesson. How do you do this?

When you only look with human eyes and listen with your human heart, you can't hear the soul talking.

Everything that you see, hear, feel, and know around you on this Earth has levels. The very lowest level of understanding is at the emotional or intuitive level. This is when you are close to the Earth, just trying to survive and constantly reacting emotionally. Most of the animal kingdom operates at this level. Humans have been given the additional ability of reasoning. So if you're willing to go a step higher and use these abilities, you push the emotions aside and say, "I'll think about it a little while." Then if you're willing to explore what's really happening as it relates to you, you have achieved a higher level of understanding. That's when you ask, "What's really going on here? I need to understand and not see with these eyes or just feel with this heart,

I need to know. I need to learn." Then you are able to see more of the picture, which allows you to see more options. You will hear the answers you need through your thoughts, conversations with others, or even in reading something. The Creator has many ways to talk to you and there is a constant dialogue going on even now.

So, if you sit around worrying all the time about other people's reactions to what you say and do, you are at an emotional level. And you're going to stay down there as long as you allow fear to control you. But if you are able to push the worrying aside and focus on what you want to learn, you are reaching a higher level. If you can further remember that when the effect comes back to you it's not really anyone's fault, it's your opportunity to change it. At that point you are reclaiming your own power and taking charge of your life. You are the creator of what's bothering you. It's not coming back for punishment; it's coming back for understanding.

The circle and cycle of learning, living, and creating is a continuous one. This means that as you come to understand and change one thing, another takes its place. You learn a little at a time.

Even once you accept the fact that you are controlling your life, it takes the rest of your life to understand how.

Every time it seems someone is hurting you or life seems to be in turmoil, you are receiving an opportunity to look at that situation and change it. All that's happening is you are constantly creating. It's energy, so it has to move. It's part of who you are, part of your spirit. The beauty about this whole thing is this circle you are enclosed in, no matter where you are in it, is perfect.

> Once you accept the fact
> that you are the creator
> of your life, it takes you
> the rest of your life to
> understand how.

Everything in Creation Has Opposites

*There really is no right or wrong, good
or bad, only opposites. Every part of
nature, including yourself, has opposites.
Both sides are needed to complete the
whole. You have a right hand and a left
hand. They do different things, but work
together to allow you to function. You have
a right eye and a left eye. They are opposites, but by working together they enable
you to see. Each performs a certain purpose in the universe. Opposites simply balance each other.*

Opposites are not just good and bad,
but actually complements of each other. It's
all in how you use them. How would you
define a description of a "good" or "bad"
thing that fits everyone and everything on

the planet? It doesn't work that way. You are each so unique and different that it would be difficult for everyone to agree. You each appoint a label of "good" or "bad" to something based on your very personal view of your whole life experiences.

Most often you use these terms "good" and "bad" when referring to the actions, thoughts, or words of each other. You also use these words when you are describing yourself. You quickly recognize the parts of yourself that you do not like and call these parts your weaker or dark side. The other side is referred to as your stronger or positive side. The reality is both sides are necessary not only to balance each other, but also to enable you to experience both pain and joy.

The Knowing vs. the Unknowing

We call these parts in you the knowing and unknowing sides. These terms have no judgment to them. The knowing part connects to your Creator and allows you to explore new thoughts and ideas. The unknowing side is afraid of change and often expresses itself through fear and anger. As we said, both sides are necessary and balance each other.

This is the key to understanding who you are. This isn't about fixing the parts of yourself you don't like. This is an acceptance that all parts of you work together.

The ultimate goal in life is to achieve a balance so you can better understand the differences on both sides. Both are necessary as you work toward a more complete understanding of who you really are.

See yourself becoming more of a whole person, not separated. Who you are at work is not separate from who you are at home. Your playtime is not separate from the moments that you spend talking to God. They are the same. They are part of the same process. Just because you get in your car and travel different places or act differently with other people does not mean that you or your life is in segments. Neither can "good" and "bad" thoughts or actions divide you.

You might ask, if there is no right or wrong, how can abuse, harm, or even murder be explained? First, it is important to understand and accept that everybody is different.

Second, the reality is that everything and everyone in the whole world are connected. You are all connected through this thing you call the soul and every living thing has one. But you are not going to respond to that connection with everyone in the same way. Each person has different characteristics and different experiences in their soul's memory. When one person commits an act such as abuse or murder, they are choosing to connect at the lowest level of understanding—the emotions. Since you have completed many life cycles on Earth, you are going to have people that you have built up very strong emotional connections with. Often they are going to be the ones that torment you the most in life. When those souls meet up again in this life, their first reaction will be the old connection of emotions. In other words, when harm is done to each other, they are simply reconnecting in the most familiar way they know. But each person involved has choices, even in those situations where it looks like they were innocent victims. What if being murdered was how they decided to die this time? Often those unjust situations affect others in such a way as to change their life. Some of the better changes within your legal system have occurred when this has happened. So that death had a purpose. It's just hard to see that purpose when humans are hurting.

Also, there's another approach to this. When you're the recipient of harmful or hurtful actions, it could very well be that the universe is using the situation to push you into a different direction. Humans tend to get satisfied with their life and be afraid to make changes. Sometimes the way to encourage change is to become miserable enough to be willing to take chances.

Is There a Heaven and Hell?

A lot of people think so because they have to justify what they have believed in or what they've done. Particularly when they think they've sinned, they want to believe in atonement. So if they are offered a set of rules to fix it, they will believe in them and try to abide by the rules. The difficulty comes in when they find it nearly impossible to do so. Therefore, they constantly need to ask for forgiveness.

Our answer would be no, there is no heaven or hell. But, as we said earlier, there have to be opposites in every part of creation. There is a place near the surface of the Earth that looks and feels like punishment because it's dark. Souls are there only because they are stuck to something or someone. They are not being punished, but choose to keep their focus on whatever it is they worship. You are worshiping something when it is on your mind most of the time. It can be a thing such as money or power, or it can be an emotion such as guilt or anger. The souls think they are stuck at this place, but they can leave any time. It's the souls' choice, but they have to be willing to let go of what's holding them.

As to a heaven, there isn't a place where

people who followed certain rules set by different religions or societies are rewarded. Instead you have the opposite of darkness, which is light. These souls are closer to the Creator only because they have released anything or anyone that could hold them back. This place of light actually is a place of reuniting, learning, and understanding.

The old question about Satan versus God has always come up. We will tell you that there is no such thing as Satan. That was created for you through old literature and it was simply trying to describe opposites and was misinterpreted. The being that you know as God is perfect, so how could anything less than perfect be part of it? Since God created opposites to make up the whole, there is a darker side to the planet and the people on it. But this darker side isn't evil, it's just the unknowing or the lack of light. If you were in a dark room you wouldn't be able to see the things around you. Are those things evil simply because they are in darkness? That is the same for those people who choose to stay in darkness.

What about Things Like War?

This isn't just about people's packages or bodies dying. The most important part is the hatred and fear inside of you that motivates you. That's what grows. There are battles on Earth because most people don't understand the power they have. They think that true power is absolute control over each other. Most of the time it's based on resources. One group or country is trying to take the resources from another. So they convince each other to be filled with hatred and anger and focus on their differences. To get humans willing to go to battle, the leaders have to convince you that you are the good side, which fights the forces of evil. They convince you that this is your purpose in life and play on fear. They have to do that in order to get you to fear or hate enough to kill.

What has happened is, in this time of communication, there has been a deliberate focus on the unknowing and not so much on the lighter side. Most people want to see pain and suffering because they're afraid of it. You think if you see more of it and understand it, you won't be so afraid of it or maybe it won't happen to you. Do not think that your whole planet is what you see or hear, because it isn't. This is not a time in history when things are darker, as you are being told.

Then why are more children being abused? Why are there more wars and killings in the streets? The truth is they have always existed; you're just hearing more about them. As we said, it causes you to focus more on the pain of others than look for the brighter side around you. What can you do about these seemingly awful things that are happening? You can take that beautiful creative power you have and send it to others in the form of love, concern, and prayers. Don't stay in the emotional part of it, the death of it, or the inhumane acts. If you feel strongly that you need to do something, then follow your instincts. For many of the people involved in these acts, it was their choice to partici- pate in order to release something that is old in them or release each other. It's important to remember that each person has the same power. They each have the same soul, connected to the same Creator. They each create their own lives and make their own choices.

How Do I Change My Thinking?

One way to change your thinking is to start to be aware of how many times in a day you say the words "good" or "bad." Look back at the end of the day and see what you were attempting to describe or define. First see that you are a complete, whole circle inside. You have a knowing side of this circle and an unknowing side of this circle. Since there is no "good" or "bad," only opposites, try to relate which side of the circle you were coming from. See if you can tell how the experience of being in the unknowing side or "bad" side helped you understand another small piece of a puzzle called living. Also, you can list the strengths you think you have and then list the weaknesses you have. Look at each one and see how they balance each other. They have to because you are a perfect being.

> **When you judge your-
> self, you strengthen
> the very parts of you
> that you dislike.**

There Are No Judgments—
Only Lessons

*Humans are the only creatures on
Earth that judge themselves. There is no
punishment or reward from God.
Everything returns to you as an opportunity to see if you want to do it the same
way or change it. How else would you
recognize it? When you judge yourself or
others, you are actually condemning your
Creator at the same time. If God is perfect and created you, was a mistake
made or could you be perfect too?*

Reward/Punishment System

In the beginning of time, when the
Creator first planted human beings on
Earth, it was important for each spirit to
recognize what he or she had created.

Consequently, the Universal Laws were included as a way for the spirit to do this. Whatever was created returned to its creator much stronger than it was originally. But when things returned to humans that involved pain or suffering, they didn't understand why and needed an explanation. Early on these basic principles were misinterpreted and human beings were left with a fear of a jealous, vengeful God. It was much easier to blame an angry God than to accept the fact that they were the creators of their own worlds. As people tried to explain punishment, the opposites were labeled as "bad" and "good" or "punishment" and "reward."

Throughout the centuries many rules have been conceived in an attempt to control one's future. That way humans could know if they were pleasing God or not by the end results that happened to them. If God answered your prayers, then you were a "good" person who followed the rules and were being "rewarded." If God didn't answer those prayers, or more "bad" things happened to you, then you were most certainly being "punished." If you needed to explain "bad" things happening to a "good" person, then obviously you were being tested by God. Over the years these rules have changed from one group to another. Different religions, societies, cultures, and even families supplied their own version of these rules from God. Most humans accept these rules as the truth even as small children. Then often you spend the rest of your life testing them.

You are told that if you live by the "right ones" you will be rewarded with success, money, and happiness. The whole idea of being a "good" person, who will be successful and happy, isn't working. So many seemingly "successful" people are still searching for something more they can hold on to. Happiness seems elusive.

To make matters worse, you've been told that when you do "bad" things, God no longer hears or is connected to you unless you beg for forgiveness. Yet these rules that you have been given to live by are so rigid that failure is inevitable. Consequently, you find yourself returning to God constantly asking forgiveness for something you have said, done, or thought. What we're saying is *God is always with you.* The Creator never went anywhere. *All God wants to do is help you recognize that you are a partner in creation.* You can't "sin" against God, but you can certainly try to pull away from Them through guilt, pain, and anger.

When you pray, you don't have to ask God to forgive you for your sins. What you can do is have a conversation with God and ask to be shown what it is you need to understand or to learn—that's it. To forgive means that you believe in a punishment system. We're saying it doesn't exist. These experiences that go in circles and come back to you are there only to make you aware of them so you can change. Fear has to be a big part of a punishment and reward system for it to work. Most of the time you're concentrating so much on the punishment, you miss seeing all the beauty around you. There is no punishment and reward, only learning experiences. Release the fear and enjoy the journey.

You will probably need to see something many times before you are able to completely let go of it. That's why you find yourself dealing with the same things over and over. If you judge yourself because of this circular way of learning, you are slowing down your own progress. You really are moving and are not in the same place you used to be. You might feel that you have stepped forward and then stepped back. What you've done is learn in your own way. Somebody else might do it a different way. Many people learn like turtles. You sit inside of your shell out of fear until you are absolutely so miserable you have nothing left to lose. Then you might stick a toe out to test and see if it works. Later you stick a leg out and finally you might stick an arm out. Eventually you poke your head, legs, and arms out to see what's there. You get to test in bits and pieces.

Judging Others

Since you are such unique beings, how you learn and how you see things will be very individual, very different. That's why it's important to share with each other but not compare. If you start comparing your life or your experiences, you're going to get in another cycle that's not very helpful. Unfortunately, that's often what humans do. They compare the material things they have, or they compare their bodies or clothes, or even compare who is the most intelligent or religious. Again, sharing your ideas, your material possessions, or your love is one thing, but to compare is to judge. Who are you really judging, you or them? If you are judging them, then you are still judging yourself because you can't see anything in them you don't already have. That can be painful because most of the things you react to in others are not things that you want to admit you have, but you do. You might think at first that you are not like the person you are reacting to and judging. But sooner or later something will happen to bring out those same reactions in you. That's the entire purpose in seeing other's imperfections; there is no judging to it.

You get stuck when you judge yourself

instead of just seeing an opportunity to change or release some old part of yourself. That's when you start adding all this extra load. It's meant to simply get your attention, to say, "Did you know that you have this in the unknowing side?" Guess what—it's a strength. You know how you call yourself "stupid" all the time or do clumsy things and fuss at yourself? That is simply a repetition of what you saw and were told growing up. It feels comforting, but it also feels miserable. If you get miserable enough, you might be willing to change that criticism to praise. You truly are the one most critical of yourself.

One way to start this change would be to see every lifetime as a stage. Each person is simply wearing a different costume and playing a different role. If you find someone in rags, that's their costume for their part of the play. Or maybe you have someone who has all the material things in life. That's their part in the play. But you get caught up in and only use those emotions that simply connect you. We aren't asking you to discount the emotions, but neither should you stay there. That's why we keep asking you to get out of them. The beauty is that all parts of the Creator are so magnificent that they can't be in just one thing. They have to be displayed and shown and lived through all kinds of things, people, and situations. To take something that beautiful and say that it can only look like this or act like that would be very limiting.

You are also each other's teachers. The people who cause you to have the strongest emotions, often not the positive ones, are your teachers. Then what are they trying to show you? Get out of the emotions and figure it out. Remember, everything goes in circles, so it's going to come back. Every time you're able to take that emotion or judgment when it comes back to you and ask, "What do I need to understand?" you literally hand yourself more power. Peace and joy take the place of the constant criticism of yourself and others. Which is why the Bible says, "Judge not that you be not judged." It's because you're judging yourself. It's not because you're going to hell if you do it, since there is no such place. But it's definitely going to come back and touch that part of you that you dislike and it becomes stronger.

Judging Yourself

It's human nature to judge yourself. You're playing a tape recorder that's inside of you and it's been there since your first minute of existence. These recordings seem to enjoy highlighting those things that resulted in harm, fear, or anger. So your recordings are going to come back automatically and say critical things to you. If you have been destitute for three lifetimes, the emotions attached to that are going to be so strong they will resurface time and time again. In turn, you might fear poverty and will do anything to keep from being poor this time. Or you might have a strong attachment to things that provide security, such as your home, money, or even food. These are the very things you are going to encounter each lifetime because you are such spiritual creatures.

Yet, when it seems your life is not working

out as you think it should, you immediately start judging yourself. You say that you didn't do this right or didn't do that right so you've failed. You haven't failed; you can't go backward. You're simply in the circle. Remember, if you are judging yourself, you are strengthening the very parts of yourself you dislike. Yet you've been trained to judge. Everything you do is either "good" or "bad" from the time you are a small child. So therefore you must be a "good" or "bad" person. It may feel good for a little while to punish yourself, but even when you call yourself "stupid" or "dumb," you are making fun of the Creator.

If you've brought with you rejection as being one of the things you fear the most, the people attracted to you will try to reject you. Which says it is simply an opportunity to learn how to get past rejection and the fear of it because you really can't reject each other. You each are powerful beings—creators. How can you accept or reject each other? Can a daisy reject a tulip? Can a pine tree reject a willow tree? No, they can't and neither can you.

Whatever fears you are trying to conquer will shape the life situations that happen to you. Let's say you have a fear of being disliked or not having money; you will probably surround yourself with people who have similar fears. Then the ones who would be judging you have the same fears. Each of you is relying on what the outward parts say—the mouth, the eyes, or body language. Start listening to your own intuition and thoughts and trust what you hear. Ask for some understanding of the situation and it will come very quickly. Usually they are not thinking what they are saying. If you will just try this when someone seems to be critical of you, it will help get you out of the emotions and into a calmer place. Know that the very thing they are doing is condemning themselves.

What looks like rejection is simply judgment turned around. They are not going to have a very strong reaction to you unless what they are judging is something that bothers them too.

Judging Your Body

One of the strongest self-criticisms we hear concerns the body. Many people feel their body, or package as we call it, is far less than perfect. They feel their bodies are the wrong color, the wrong size, or the wrong shape. First, you pretty much chose your body style when you chose your parents and your lifestyle before each lifetime. Second, we would like you to think of the body as a package, a covering. That's all it is. It houses the soul or the spirit and it's like wearing a costume on stage while in a play. Does the costume tell you who or what the actor wearing it really is? No. It's only necessary to help them with their part in that particular play. Once the play is over and you die, the costume will come off as the spirit continues on.

Another way to look at it would be if you went to a party where there were boxes all wrapped in different wrappings, all different sizes, with different colors of bows and trims. These differences are so much more pleasing to the eye than ten boxes all the same size and wrapped just alike. So it is with your packages, as far as the Creator's concerned. Don't ever condemn yourself for the package you are in. Each person is unique. Why would God want to look at a field of flowers that are exactly the same? Anyway, the things about you that you dislike the most are the very things the Creator knows you by. The very weaknesses you detest are your strengths.

Remember also that the body is a place that stores the soul, the logic or the mind, the heart, and the emotions. All these parts work together. When the soul is distressed, physical problems can occur. When there is a lot of emotion or distress, it will go to the weakest part of the body. Many of the diseases known today are due to strong emotions sitting in the body with nowhere to go. If you have pain and suffering, the body is trying to get your attention and let you know that something is going on you need to be aware of and change.

Each person comes with a mission and a purpose to their life. Their mission is how they choose to contribute toward mankind as a whole. Their purpose is the individual things that soul chooses to understand and accomplish in the lifetime. What the bottom line comes to, that you're not being told, is that you get to feel good when you do both.

Explaining Relationships

Sometimes it's hard not to judge someone who is doing or saying something meant to hurt you. Usually your first tendency is to just react to them. When this happens, it's usually someone you've connected with before in previous lives, and both of you have this agreement that you don't remember. You both agree to do certain things to each other so you both can remember what you've forgotten. It's one way to remember what you want to try and change in this lifetime.

That's why you get into relationships. That's why you have people you know who drive you crazy. Why else would you do such harmful things to each other? Let's say that you have had numerous past life experiences where several people have treated you very badly. There's a very good chance that you will indeed meet up with those people again, because you were drawn to them originally by emotions. They're brought back into the circle by emotions. It's as though a magnet pulls you both together, even though you don't realize you're doing it. The tendency is to repeat the same old pattern that is very familiar unless you understand what is going on. The same misery or whatever you felt before will be there again. Many people get very comfortable with that misery, because they think that's all there is.

When you're in these experiences, it's part of the circle. It is not punishment. It is not something you're doing wrong. It's an opportunity.

Nothing is ever what it seems to be at first glance. There's always more to it.

All you have to do to change the situation is to change yourself. You don't have to deal with the other person, just look at yourself. That other person will be affected in some way by your changes and will probably be released. All you're together for is to learn. But be aware that as you try to change yourself, the other people around you might become resentful. People tend to become upset when they can't expect the same responses from you that they've always had. This resentment comes because they can't control you any longer. When you change how you respond to them, they will be forced to change how they react to you.

Sometimes your intuition warns you early in the relationship, but you have a way of rationalizing and discounting the behavior. When the relationship becomes destructive you might start out blaming others, but usually you end up criticizing yourself. You think that if you just do this or that differently, things will be great. You've been working very hard to show them love, and yet you can't understand why they want to return it with harm. To regain what's truly yours, all you have to do is start to be aware of your "flaws" and learn to love them.

Society tends to criticize couples when relationships break up. The couples even criticize themselves. Often people don't understand why they get involved in a number of relationships. They think they are a failure. What you really are doing is simply agreeing to be each other's teacher. If one person is stuck at one place in life, another person comes along and says, "Hey, remember me? Let's go on further up the path and look at this together." You might be in that relationship for a day or years and then decide to move on or go in a different direction. You haven't failed at a marriage, but just decided you had completed whatever was needed with that person. Even if you can't actually recognize that at the time, you can know that something pushed you to get out of the relationship and back onto your own path. You jolt each other like that. It's a plan that works very well if you can get rid of judgment that takes place.

Lessons

Everything we have spoken of is a learning process. When you were young, you didn't get the multiplication table the first time you tried it. You had to keep on doing it until you had it memorized. At some point in frustration you probably said, "Why do I need this?" It probably was much later in life that you realized it had a purpose. Maybe it was the first time you tried to balance your checkbook or needed to know how to make change. This whole process we are talking about is the same, except it's about awareness. Instead of criticizing yourself or others for your "mistakes," see it as being in school and simply reciting the multiplication table. You practice it over and over and at some point you accomplish it and the purpose for each experience will come clear to you.

These lessons give you an opportunity to use both parts of yourself, the knowing and unknowing. The more that you can understand and accept both parts of you, the more perfect you become within your own life. Then the less you are looking for that kind of perfection in anybody else. Now that means the person driving by you on the freeway is also perfect, as well as the person sitting next to you at work. If you are having angry feelings about them or yourself, it's going to affect that other part of God going down the road. That's how you are all connected.

How Do You Change?

It helps if you can start to see your world and everything in it, including yourself, as beings who have to contain opposites. It takes both parts to be perfect. Start to become aware of how often you categorize things or people as "good" or "bad." Be aware of the times you are judging others and certainly yourself. Changes come in stages. You become aware of a new concept and you go out, even if it's subconsciously, and test it. You can know you are testing it when your teachers for that particular subject appear in your life. Only when you experience that test for yourself are you going to know if it is true or not.

Also be aware of what you ask for. If you've asked for more patience, you're going to have more people around that irritate you. They are your teachers for patience.

Otherwise, how would you learn? Everybody is on Earth to learn certain things. The only way it's going to change is in little pieces. It isn't going to just go away all at once. You have to do a little bit each day. During the day, stop and take small mental breaks. We're talking to you all the time and you can check on yourself.

You might go a day or even a week feeling really good. Then, a problem appears or turmoil hits and that's where you get stuck. You think, "Okay, now I've failed and I've got to start all over." No! This process is a circle, so it's got to come back around, doesn't it? That's all you're doing. You're revisiting the same circles in order to release it a little at a time. Then you get geared back up and the next time you are able to see a little sooner that turmoil or problems are opportunities. After a while you won't hang on to it so long because you won't be interested in it anymore. Then, instead of judging yourself, you will see more and more pieces of yourself that are perfect.

**We all have angels
to help us. Their main
duty is simply to love us.**

Your Angels

*You have all the help you need while
trying to figure all of this out. Everyone
has angels. We chose to be with you. You
didn't earn us, so you can't lose us even
in death. We know your every thought,
word, or deed in every life. We are talking to you constantly and want to help
you with information, decisions, and
protection. Our ultimate job, though, is
to simply love you.*

Duties

We are as connected to you as your fingers, your mouth, or your ears. Consequently,
we hear and know everything you say,
think, and do. Even the Bible tells you to be
aware that there are angels all around you

and nothing is done in secret. Just as your feet have the duty to carry you around, we have duties. We were created because the Creator was a little concerned about each one of you and thought you might need a little help. Since you didn't do anything to earn us, you can't get rid of us or push us away.

One of our main purposes for being here is to simply love you. In that loving we attempt to show you how beautiful you really are, because you have forgotten. It is going to be hard for you to understand and remember this in a human body. Yet, that is our very foremost duty and it really isn't difficult for us.

Most children are aware of our existence. You talk to us by calling us imaginary friends. But somewhere in between childhood and adulthood, you are told we don't exist or won't help you. So you believe that we only appear in your lives occasionally as miracles. There is no miracle to it. It's just that on those occasions you were able to recognize us and know that you had help with that particular problem or trauma. We are working with you every minute of every day, not just when things seem to be falling apart.

All humans have at least one or two angels that have been with them since the beginning of time. Each of us has various duties we have agreed to do. For instance, one might be in charge of keeping you alive and protecting you. Another might help with your work or relationship problems. If you have a difficult task in front of you, there might be others who come in to help for a while.

God vs. Angels

You might be wondering what our relationship is to you and God. If you are talking to us, are you ignoring God? We are as much a part of the Creation as you are, and we also are a part of each one of you. By that very question you are trying to separate these parts of creation. You are taught from infancy that you are separate from each other by age, sex, race, culture, and religion. You are also taught that God is way up in heaven and separate from you. The truth is there is nothing you can do or say that can separate you from each other, from nature, or from God. Sometimes various religions have put themselves in the position of being your mediator to God. They want you to let them talk to God for you. At gatherings they tell you God's message along with God's rules. That way of thinking gives them the power that is rightfully yours.

Another way to look at this relationship would be for you to look at your hands. Does the right hand know what the left one's doing? Probably not, but they still automatically work together. Know that angels are very much like that. They are your hands, your ears, or your mouth. Anyone talking to angels is automatically talking to the Creator. In fact, God knows all of your conversations as well as your thoughts. So if you think you have to pray specifically to God, They already know what the prayer is. Some people would be very uncomfortable with the thought that God hears and sees you all the time. Yet know that at the same time the Creator doesn't judge you.

So the answer to the question is, there is

no separation in creation. We say that we are all part of one consciousness. There's an all-inclusive oneness. If you hit your toe on something and hurt it, the rest of your body will feel the pain and respond to protect it. That's how you are with God. You are so incorporated. We can't say that the Creator is just in this little tiny spot way up in heaven or in your heart. The Creator is in every cell of your body and you can't separate yourself from them. Yet that's what others are trying to do.

What is prayer? Prayer is connection, but so are conversation and experiences. It's just one form of connecting to your Creator. Humans touch, hug, do things for each other, and speak to each other. You connect to each other in lots of ways. Likewise you have many ways of connecting with God. You are connecting with God when you stop to enjoy a sunset. You are connecting when you are unselfish or kind. So conversation with your Creator is just another way to connect. You don't even have to start the prayer in any particular way at all. You truly are conversing as soon as you have a thought or open your mouth, whether you are directing it that way or not.

Why Can't You See Angels?

You're probably wondering, if we exist then why can't you see us. Usually it's fear or disbelief that stops you. Maybe it's the fear of what you'll see. Maybe it's the fear if you don't see us, this whole thing is a hoax and then what are you supposed to believe? Also, if you think seeing us is impossible, then you have limited any opportunity you might have to actually accomplish that.

Trying to see us with the naked eye can be difficult. You have to train, not your two eyes, but the third eye that is located right between the eyes, in the middle of the forehead. That's what you see with. Your regular eyes will deceive you, the other won't. You do this by starting to be very conscious of the fact that angels are with you. Just about everyone has seen something they couldn't explain in their lifetime; they just didn't know what it was. Recognize, too, that someone decided to draw an angel eons ago and that's what you think we're supposed to look like. We don't. Actually our light is so brilliant it would blind you if you did see us directly with your two eyes. But don't expect to see wings and halos.

Communication

If you can learn to communicate with us when you are awake, your life will be easier. The most natural way to talk to you is through your own thoughts, or the mind. It was the original way of communicating. The mouth was added as an afterthought for humans to be able to feed the body, not necessarily to communicate. Since we've been talking to you through your own thoughts from the beginning, it's difficult for you to separate your thoughts from our words. Everyone has heard us speak to them. You just believed it was your own thoughts.

The way to start hearing us is to ask us a question. If it is directed specifically to us, the very next thought in your head is our answer. Often it takes a lot of practice to be able to trust that what you are hearing is our reply. Just about everyone has had a thought that seemed to "come out of the blue." That usually is your angels talking to you. When we speak, it will be one quiet, calm thought, not lots of excited chatter.

How can you know that it is your angels talking and not just what you want to hear? The parts of you that cause all the confusion are the old tapes. As we said earlier, you have a tape recorder inside of your mind that has been recording everything from your very first second of existence. These tapes recorded every thought, belief, or feeling you ever had. There was no editing of what was logical or reasonable. These old tapes are going to be the old patterns that go through your thoughts most often. They'll feel comfortable or familiar even if they are hurtful or destructive ones.

The tape recorder was put there in case you got lost. You would at least have some memories of past lives to help guide you. Usually those old patterns are the very things you are here to change, so you need to have them happen over and over. For many people it's the only source of memory they have to rely on. You tend to use that tape recorder much more than anything else. That's the most familiar, so you simply repeat these beliefs without question. Or even if you question the pattern, you feel you have no power to change it. You don't realize that the answers are right inside your own mind. That's why we sound like you. Quite often we introduce a new solution to an old belief right along with your thinking patterns. We do it gently so as not to frighten you.

Communicating through Dreams

Dreaming is another way of communicating, whether you're awake or asleep. Most people have had daydreams and sometimes we can help in those. Where do you think your dreams come from? We are simply reminding you of old accomplishments or new possibilities. Obviously, we can do a whole lot more with you in your sleep than we can with daydreaming. When you are going to sleep, the first part of your dreams will be connected to the very last minutes or hours before you go to bed. Sometimes you take your worries or your unfinished work with you into your dreams. If you've had a busy day and the body is exhausted, the mind sits there and argues with us for half the night. That makes it difficult for us to communicate. If you were watching a horror movie or even the news before bedtime, you will take some of that with you. That's the first part of your dreams and tends to set the direction for the entire night. Dreaming is like going into a corridor and the last bit of memory before you go to bed determines which door you will take.

Your worries or your tasks distract your attention. Combine those things with the emotions that come with them and you can wake up feeling even more distressed and tired. The very best way to handle problems is to ask us for our help in understanding them and changing them. In order to communicate clearly, it helps to have your mind clear when you go to sleep.

All humans originally came from different

places, planets, and universes. We were simply conceived with you. We have been with you from the first moment and will stay with you until you see your total perfection. We want to help you with all things in life but mostly we just want to love you.

The key to being perfect
is not to try and fix
the things you don't like
about yourself, but
to accept all parts
as being necessary.

Perfection

What do you think perfect feels like or looks like? Where is it? Is it something that you can get now or is it a reward of some sort? Perfect isn't a place or the end result of being a good person; it's a state of mind. What if your life is filled with thousands of perfect moments and after your death you discover you've missed them? Would you recognize a perfect moment in your life right now?

What Is Perfect?

When we are talking about the concept of being perfect, what picture do you have in your head? What are you expecting it to be? Do you think it would be a constant state of blissfulness and you would always have everything you need? We want to stop you if that is the picture you have in your mind. That kind of thinking only acknowledges one side of creation. It doesn't allow room for anything but joy and peace. Even though you can't fully comprehend what that would feel like, it wouldn't be what you think. Your existence would get pretty boring after a few centuries of experiencing the same thing every day.

Remember the last time you felt anxious or worried about something and then everything worked out in the end and you were so relieved? Or maybe you had a disagreement with someone and were hurt only to make up later and feel that rush of joy? It is impossible to understand joy and peace if you haven't experienced pain and suffering. Perfection is the understanding and acceptance of both parts of yourself and your life. It's the knowing and unknowing.

All the laws that we have given up to this point help you understand this. If you can understand and accept the first law that says, "You are creating your life," then you obviously are the one in control of whether or not you get perfection. Since there is no reward or punishment, you can't earn perfection on Earth or in heaven. If you accept that you are creating your life in circles, then you know what you create returns to you. The return is only to help you see and change the parts you don't like. This enables you to release reward and punishment. So the only thing that stops you from accepting perfection is your idea of what it's supposed to look and feel like.

Another law we have presented to you states that for anything to be complete there have to be opposites. There's no way around that. When your life feels out of control, you call it chaos. For example, it could be feeling unhappiness, anger, or hurt. It could be that your life isn't measuring up to your expectations. This chaos or the unknowing feels like you are in a dark room with the lights off. What we are trying to do is get you to be more comfortable in that darkness.

The more you venture out of your comfortable area (from the knowing to the unknowing), the more uncomfortable it's going to feel. The more it's going to look frightening and dark. Now what does that mean in your everyday living? Let's take an example. Let's say that you are a big, brown bear in a zoo. To you life has been perfect. You were born there, so zoo life is all that you know. You are familiar with every inch of the caged area and you feel safe behind the bars. You have water to play in and caves to sleep in. You get fed regularly and have all your friends and family around you. What more could you want? Life seems perfect. You have your routine and know what's going to happen day after day.

But inside of you is a little voice that wonders what it's like outside of those bars. When you ask the older bears, they tell you it's bad to question, that it's scary. You just don't know what's going to happen out there. You have no guarantee of being fed. There are even people out there who could hurt you. But in spite of their warnings, there is still this part of you that wants to see for yourself. After a while the knowing can get very boring.

Many people spend their entire lives trying to stay in their cages. You purposely work at the same jobs, live in the same area, stay with the same people, eat the same food, wear the same clothes, and watch the same TV. These people are very afraid of change and they like being inside of those bars. You feel secure and in control of your life because you pretty much know the routine. But inside each of you is a little voice that longs to explore or fulfill your mission and purpose for being here. That's the part which pulls you into the unknowing and makes you uncomfortable or miserable at best. That is the thing that pulls you outside of that cage.

The bear, while he is safe in his cage at the zoo, thinks it's perfect. To think otherwise, he has to get discouraged enough to start to see what's around him with different eyes. This means you usually have to get pretty miserable to be willing to take a chance or go beyond those bars. If you are perfectly happy then you aren't even going to be interested in trying. Usually you see others around you in their misery first before you will acknowledge that you could be unhappy. Most humans make a considerable effort to try and convince each other that they have a perfect life. Let's say you are one of the bears left in the cage. It's going to make you very uncomfortable to see your friend or loved one on the outside. Then you have to choose to stay in your cage or try to get out with them.

Usually humans do not see the freedom that comes to those who actually make the change. Instead you focus on the chaos and stay in the pain of it all. If you are inside the cage watching those outside the cage, you only see their fear, not their bravery. It's also hard to see somebody that you love in misery. Your first impulse is to try and fix it for them. The reality is that you can't fix it for them. But you certainly can be grateful, because that means they have chosen to go through a change. Good! Let them do it and don't try to stop it, fix it, or change it. Let them be miserable and see them as the strong beings they truly are. They aren't alone; they have all the help they need.

Misery is part of the human experience of learning. It's one of the things that will get you out of that cage. Maybe some of the other bears start picking on you or the zoo serves the same food for ten years and you get tired of it. Maybe the water will dry up or you will tire of people gawking at you, whatever it is. Suddenly perfect isn't perfect anymore. That is one of the first steps in change. That gets you to a place where you are willing to go explore, and it is going to feel scary.

What do you think it would feel like when that brown bear finally escapes from his or her cage? Do you think that he would feel absolutely terrified when he first gets out? Probably he would. Change is terrifying. It is the unknowing, because that bear does not know what is going to happen next. His world is in chaos and he doesn't even know where to go or where the next meal is coming from. He doesn't know if there's anybody else out there to be with him. That bear just knows that he had to get out and see for himself.

Once the fear subsides, out of necessity the bear starts exploring the area around the zoo. Eventually he goes a few blocks from the zoo and finds an old garage and over time gets comfortable. He might find food in the garbage cans, make friends with a few cats, and start to create a home in that garage. There's an excitement to exploring and overcoming the challenge. That is how you discover how powerful you are. If you never take the challenge, you won't know for sure if you can do it. No longer is the bear in the unknowing. Instead the unknowing is a little way beyond the garage. So when that bear gets uncomfortable enough or miserable enough to try again, he will be ready to venture further.

This is exactly what happens to you. The more you are willing to open up to change, the more uncomfortable it feels. There is a part of you that naturally is going to be afraid. It may say, "Oh my God, where is my next meal coming from or what will my friends think or what am I going to do because my life has changed so dramatically?" All that tells you is that you are in the process of making what was before unknowing into the knowing. When we say that each person is perfect, we're saying that you are whole. It doesn't matter if you are operating from your knowing part or unknowing part.

Start to accept the fact that perfect is what you are now, whether you are using it to your benefit or not. Consequently, everything that happens to you is there to help you understand more of the unknowing side of you for your benefit. The more you are willing to get out of that zoo and take chances, the more you will understand how these laws work. More often than not, these golden opportunities are seen as punishment.

Everybody can talk, but doing it is another matter. The people who make fun of you are the ones watching. The ones who criticize you are the ones *really* watching. So if you are getting lots of criticism at this point in your life, you've got a pretty good audience out there. There are times to share some information, but on the whole they aren't ready to listen. They would prefer to watch you instead. And indeed, by watching you change they will learn in spite of themselves.

We want you to become used to the idea

of being perfect now. This is not a reward that you get after you've accomplished ten tasks. This is not a reward you get after twenty lifetimes. You are getting what you call the reward now. When are you willing to accept it? We really don't have such a word as perfect in our world; we don't need it. For us it is simply being. So accepting your perfection is about reuniting yourself, each other, and your very personal connection to God. If you can do it in small pieces, a little each day, then at some point you will get a larger picture of what whole and complete really means. So when you are looking at what perfect feels like, know that it can happen right now because it's inside of you. It's not where you go, what you have, what you do, or even how much chaos is in your life. It is simply how you choose to view your life. So what are you working on today? What did you figure out? You can know that things are working when you feel at peace—and each time it's going to get stronger.

The truth doesn't change, it just changes us.

All Your Paths Lead to the Same Place

This experience you call life is really a classroom. Everyone graduates eventually. Since you get to create your life one day at a time, and there are no judgments in the process, only lessons, the whole classroom is for your own discovery. You get to enjoy the trip because all paths lead to the Creator anyway.

How Do You Know This Is True?

Our answer to that question would be, "Try it and see for yourself." Just look at the first law and see how you are creating your life. Take a small step and create your day by those first thoughts in the morning. See if you feel the changes from day to day. Your life won't be without problems, but they won't have as much control over you. You will slowly realize that you are in charge of creating your life, with all the power of the universe at your disposal. In the process you get to take more pleasure in those people and places around you.

Love is the most powerful force in existence. What we're trying to do is teach you to love yourself, first. It's not just important; it's essential. Until you discover what we already know about who you truly are, how are you going to be able to show that to other people? (We said *show*, not just tell.) It's through your life experiences that you discover this. As you find yourself struggling, the changes in your life will affect others. As you learn to love more of yourself, you are teaching others how to do the same. That is why this is so important. As you discover new and exciting parts of yourself, you are going to touch hundreds of people every day without even knowing it.

How Is This Different?

What is the difference between this and what you have heard from others? First, we are reminding you that you have the power over your life. You get to make the choices. When you make a decision that doesn't feel right for you, there is no punishment. There's only the law that says all things go in circles and are simply returning to you. You will not go to a place that you call hell if you make a "mistake." Hell doesn't exist. That also means you can let go of the labels of "right" and "wrong" or "good" and "bad." Instead, you can start to see your life as a continual process of exploring. One path might be short; yet another could be really long. One could have briars everywhere and you think you are stuck. Upon closer examination, there could be fruit on those briars and you get to enjoy them. It's the same path and the same briars; it's all how you view it.

We also are saying that you don't have to accomplish ten steps to reach perfection—you're already there. If you choose to stay in one place for a while, repeating the same situations, it is your choice. You will learn in that place just as well as if you were traveling along at a great speed. So there is no one true path. Each person gets to make as many trips on different paths as they wish. They all reach home eventually.

We are also saying that you each are supposed to be unique and different. Everyone isn't supposed to like the same things or see things the same way. If you were a pottery maker and you made fifty coffee cups, no two coffee cups would look alike. The way you made them is probably going to be pretty similar, yet they're going to turn out different. The differences may be very small, but they will be there.

You each have within your very soul or spirit, a portion of the Creator that is the same—just like the clay in the coffee cups. So you each share common spiritual DNA from your Creator, but you were still created with different colors, shapes, and sizes. Each person has different gifts and abilities, even if they share families, looks, or even life. That makes you unique. Since you are supposed to be different, judgment of others is unnecessary. How can you decide what is best for someone else? Do you know all there is to know about them? Are you aware of all of their lives and what they hope to accomplish this lifetime? Of course you also get to stop judging yourself in the process.

Most all messages have some truth to them. But if if someone's message says that theirs is the only way to reach understanding, that is too rigid and narrow. If anyone tells you that you will be punished if you don't do things a certain way and you don't have choices, then be aware that is not true. You always have choices and different ways of learning. If anyone says only they can give God's message, be aware. Talk to God yourself and see. Does the information leave you feeling peaceful or guilty? Is it giving you back your power or trying to take yours by claiming to have more knowledge than you do? One thing we have said consistently is that everyone has this power; we're simply reminding you. You already have everything you need.

We are also saying that you are only responsible for yourself. The truth is that you really can't take care of anybody else.

You've got your hands full with yourself. What you can do is share with each other. That's it. You cannot go out there and fix anyone. When you have the idea in your head that you're responsible for someone else (except children), that statement in itself says, "I'm stronger, you're weaker, so I really need to take care of you because you obviously can't do it for yourself."

Think about that. That's the message you are giving them. Is that really helping them? How can young children learn to ride bikes by themselves if you are always holding on? At some time you have to let go and just know they can do it. They may fall several times, but they have to learn on their own how to do it. You can turn that around and say: "You have power, too. What I choose to do is see you as strong, so you can do this for yourself." Then you are giving them the greatest gift in the universe.

Going Home

There has been planted in each soul a seed that says, "I remember being part of the 'Great I AM' and being whole and complete. I want to go back." There is a part of you that wants to go home. It's a part that is looking for something much bigger and grander than yourself. Everybody's ideas of what home looks like are very different. How you get there is going to be different also.

You're here to remember and have a good time doing it. You are also here to meet people and create memories. The only things you can take with you when you die are the memories of that lifetime. You will come to a point when you will remember them all, but that usually doesn't happen until you are reviewing your lives.

You get to experience something and then, having been through it, take it with you. That's why we say what you take with you when you die is what is in that tape recorder in your memory. You get to experience life firsthand, which is so important. For instance, if you were watching a program on TV about rafting down a river, your heart might start to pound a little as you imagine what that would be like. If, however, you actually were rafting down a river, your reactions and memories would be considerably stronger and clearer. The experience of living in a body on Earth enhances those memories you take with you. So celebrate, you are a whole, perfect being connected to God and others. You will reach home no matter what the path or the speed you are traveling.

Epilogue

These laws are not to be considered the same as we have traditionally known laws to be. There is no punishment to these laws. These are the blueprints of the universe, or simply guideposts to help you on your journey. You will not be able to use this book to your best advantage if you see them as steps that you have to accomplish. It's sort of like staring at a stop sign while you are driving and missing the stop altogether. It's all in how you see it. Each law is simply given to help you understand the inner workings within the order of the universe.

This is not another book telling you to do steps one through eight correctly and you will be given a perfect score. First, it is not a test, and second, there are no steps, just circles. It took me many years to unlearn what I had been taught about breaking rules and the consequences. As a preacher's daughter, most of the philosophy in life that I was taught was based on guilt or fear. One of my strengths that drove everyone crazy was my inability to just accept things. I questioned everything with some cynicism. I especially drove teachers crazy in school. Even when I was in graduate school in my early forties, I questioned everything I was told. It doesn't make you the popular one on campus. Yet, that caution has helped me eliminate a host of baggage that I could have carried around this lifetime.

Try to see this book as very similar to looking at the blueprints of a building or a car or even a toy. Each piece fits together for it to work. One example would be like when our dishwasher at home was broken many years ago. I was going to school, working, and trying to run a household. The last thing I needed was a broken dishwasher. So, I proceeded to take the thing apart to try to fix it. I didn't think it could be that difficult. Since I had no earthly clue how those things worked other than how to fill with cleanser and start it, I made it much worse. Eventually, we had to pay someone to come and repair my mess. The problem wasn't my willingness to attempt it, but my lack of knowledge as to how dishwashers are put together.

Most people have purchased something that had to be assembled at one time or another and, without fail, some part was missing from the kit. It makes for a frustrating time. But the truth is we are all wandering around every day trying to make sense out of our lives without all of the instructions; pieces seem to be missing. Even once we think we have everything we need, we have to stop and read and reread the directions before we are able to put things together. Now, I'm one of those people who hate taking the time to read the instructions to something. Whether it is directions to baking a new dessert or building a fence, I don't like to take the time to read those directions. More often than not, I end up having to go back and figure them out because I messed up.

I don't read the instructions because I'm usually in a hurry and I'd like to think I could do it my own way. The truth is I am reluctant to admit that someone else could possibly know better than I do the inner workings of their own creation. The fact is they do and I'm not giving up anything by taking the time to use those instructions properly. Once done, I can use whatever it is I'm attempting to put together for my own advantage. These guidelines are simply trying to tell you how the system of order works for this and all the other universes. They are trying to show you how you can use them to your own benefit. Read them and then reread them. Once you start putting the pieces together, you will see how it all works. And it does work, I assure you.

I have run most of my life from who I really am. Sure, it's been helpful to see and talk to my angels, but I still have had long periods in my life where I felt alone and very confused. *Knowing* all the principles in this book won't change your life; you have to *use* them to understand them. Only after many trials will you begin to understand how powerful your thoughts are. Once you get the toy or whatever you are building put together, you need to *use* it to get the full benefit. It does you no good just sitting on a shelf. That's where many people get stuck. They read a book, get excited, maybe try a new thing or two, then put it up and move on to something else. I know, because I've done it myself. There are only a very few books that I return to over and over again to help me with everyday situations.

People I meet are amazed. They think that if I can see and talk to dead people and angels, and can go to the past and the future, what problems could I possibly have? The truth is, I have had to learn my lessons just like everyone else, the hard way. It took many years to trust that what I saw and heard were indeed my angels. It also took many years to acknowledge to others what I am capable of. I certainly haven't arrived and am still in the process of learning how to love myself more. But I can assure you that if you are willing to use this book to let go of old ways of thinking a little piece at a time, your life will become more peaceful even in the face of seeming disaster.

Before I started writing this book, I was the director of a small nonprofit organization that worked with people who had been sexually abused and involved in domestic violence. It took most of my time, but provided some very interesting personal lessons. My own angels told me that I would need to quit and start writing. We had just bought a house and my husband is a self-employed writer/photographer. So this was not great news. We certainly weren't independently wealthy.

I put it off and the more I did the tighter our funds became. My paychecks no longer paid the bills. So finally I listened and quit. Immediately the funds came to us and they haven't stopped. I was told we would be taken care of and we have been. They have come from various sources, but they still came. The lesson is, you can fight whatever is in front of you, but all you'll do is get tired. Fighting is not what powerful people do. They do everything within reason, then they simply release the situation and go on about their business. It works out beautifully every time if we just take our sticky fingers off of it.

I can say that my life is filled with perfect moments. It may be playing with my absolutely beautiful granddaughter. It may be sharing ordinary moments with my husband, children, or friends. It may be playing in the flower gardens around our home. Whatever it is and whenever they come, I am constantly reminded of just how perfect I am becoming.

About the Author

By the time she was six years old, B.J. Wall realized that she was able to see and hear angels and the dead, but it was many years before she understood her ability.

In the intervening years she married her soul mate, an author/photographer whose work with Native Americans introduced the author to many medicine men and women who shared with her their friendships as well as their customs and beliefs.

Wall earned a master's degree in counseling in order to combine the metaphysical with the professional in her healing work. After eighteen years of providing spiritual counseling, healing, and teaching, she has recorded the truth she has heard from her angels in *The Handbook for Perfect Beings*. Its companion, *The Guidebook for Perfect Beings*, provides an intimate look at the author's experiences.

The author and her husband live near Richmond, Virginia, where they can be close to their growing family, which now includes grandchildren. She recently started the Fellowship of Perfect Beings Church and continues to teach, counsel, and write.